Under the Sea 16

A Stormy Day 18

The World's Seas 20

The Water Cycle 22

Index 24

A Busy River

Big rivers are lively places. Watch one for a while, and you'll see pleasure boats cruising to and fro, and cargo ships returning to port.

The river too is on the move. Its journey started a long way from the city, and has already taken several days.

5

Where a River Starts

Rivers start on hilltops and mountain peaks. Here, there is so much rain and snow that water is always trickling down the hillside.

One tiny trickle leads into another. Slowly, they grow into a stream of clear, fresh water that picks up speed and flows quickly on its way.

Faster and Faster

As the bubbling streams flow into one another, the river grows bigger and gathers pace. It races down the hillside, snatching up small stones and pebbles. They swirl around in the water, chipping away at the banks and river bed.

Over thousands of years, this pounding and chipping carves a valley into the hillside.

The river flows very quickly

9

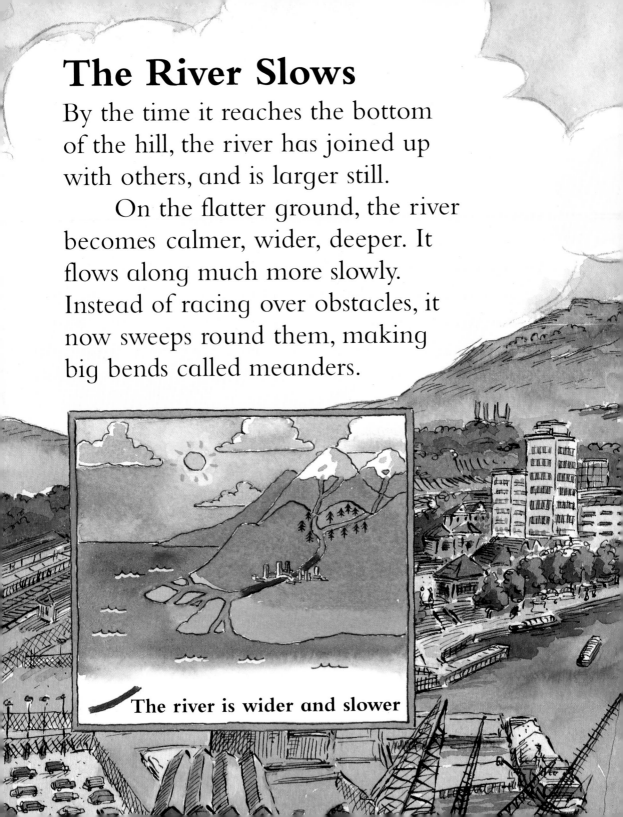

The River Slows

By the time it reaches the bottom of the hill, the river has joined up with others, and is larger still.

On the flatter ground, the river becomes calmer, wider, deeper. It flows along much more slowly. Instead of racing over obstacles, it now sweeps round them, making big bends called meanders.

The river is wider and slower

Journey's End

The river ends its journey at the sea. By now, it is moving so slowly that the mud and stones it was carrying sink down to the river bed, and pile up into mudflats. The gooey mud is teeming with snails, shellfish and wriggly worms – a delicious feast for seabirds!

The river's mouth

13

The Salty Sea

Not far from the river's mouth lies the open sea. The air is fresher here, with the tangy smell of salt.

The sea is vast. It stretches much further than our eyes can see. Twice a day it rises up the beach, and then it falls – leaving a tangle of seaweed and sticks on the high tide line.

15

Under the Sea

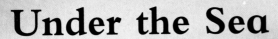

Along the coast, dry land slopes
down into the sea. The water here
is shallow, light and warm.
Colourful fish hide in the seaweed
and dart among the rocks.

Far out from the shore, the
seabed slopes down steeply. The
water is deeper, cold and dark,
with fewer plants and animals.

A Stormy Sea

The sea is never still. On calm days, gentle ripples break lazily on the shore. But on windy days, dark waves tower over the fishing boats, and fling them up and down.

Waves are made as the wind blows across the water. The stronger the wind, the bigger the waves!

➤ **The wind blows this way**

The World's Seas

Most of the Earth is covered in salty seawater. Look at a map, and you'll see that four blue oceans stretch between the biggest pieces of land. They are the Pacific, Atlantic, Indian and Arctic Oceans. The Pacific alone covers more of the Earth's surface than all the land put together!

Pacific Ocean

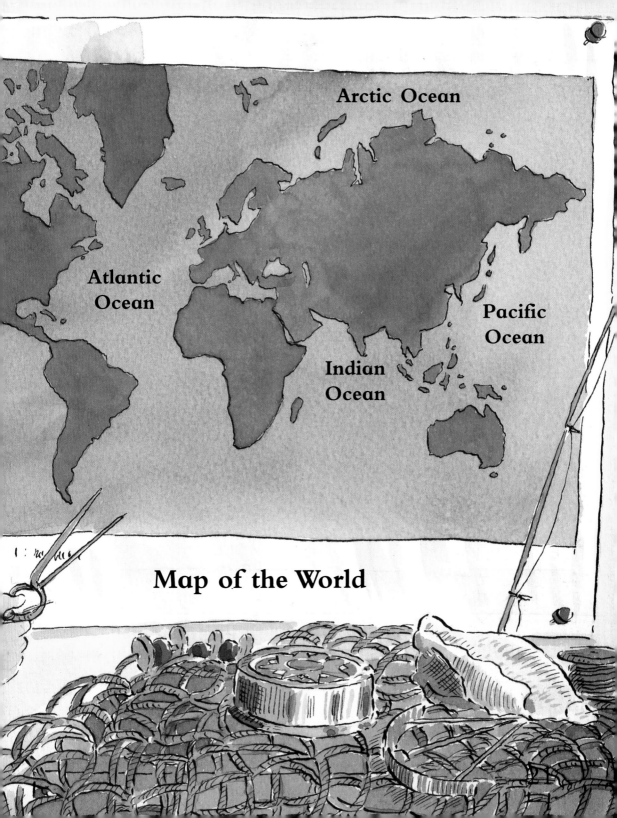

Arctic Ocean

Atlantic
Ocean

Pacific
Ocean

Indian
Ocean

Map of the World

The Water Cycle

The oceans play an important part in the world's weather. The Sun's heat makes water evaporate from the sea. As the water vapour rises in the sky, it cools, and forms clouds. Their rain feeds the rivers that flow to the sea.

The world's water moves in a never-ending circle from the land and sea to the sky. We call this the water cycle.

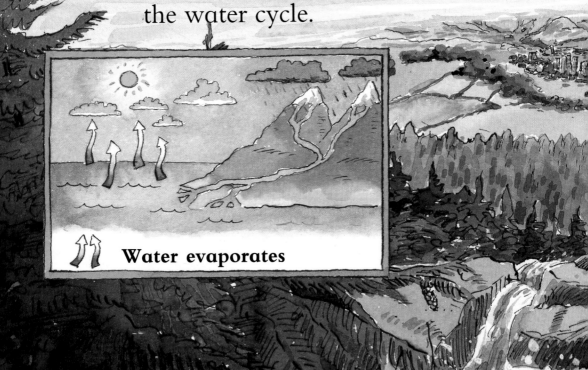

Water evaporates

Index

beach 14
boats 4, 18

clouds 22
coast 16

land 16, 20, 22

meander 10
mudflats 12

rain 6, 22
river bed 8
river mouth 12, 14

seabed 16
seaweed 14, 16
ships 4
shore 16, 18
stream 6, 8
Sun 22

valley 8

water 6, 8, 16, 18, 22
water vapour 22
waves 18
weather 22
wind 18